tropical
minimal

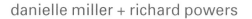
danielle miller + richard powers

tropical
minimal

Thames & Hudson

contents

introduction
the simply tropical lifestyle

Minimalism and the sultry clarity of the tropics go hand in hand.

By eliminating all superfluous clutter, you can achieve natural order,

calm and tranquillity.

Sit back, relax and feel the essence of summer in a place that is entirely in tune with your surroundings, a place that responds to your emotions and sense of well-being. That enables you to slow down to feel the sun, the rain and the breeze. That leaves lasting impressions as you reflect on what nature intended through a seamless, minimal divide. From the sleek refinement of an urban dwelling to the sensual approach of a jungle retreat, interiors, exteriors and outdoor rooms reveal unique expressions in entirely creative ways. Pared down to the essentials, without fuss and with nothing extraneous to detract from the allure of life in the tropics.

In this entrance in São Paulo, designed by Isay Weinfeld, a cool composition is given a vibrant injection of colour with an isolated and unexpected splash of yellow.

As anyone who has ever seen the effusive sights of the scenery and the surreal brilliance of the light, the colour, the ocean, and the open sky will agree, there is something enigmatic and intangibly exotic about the tropics. Perhaps it is simply in the year-round companionable warmth of the climate, the genuine friendliness of the people and their laid-back lifestyle. Here the simple desire to be out in the open provides the perfect opportunity and the freedom for design and architecture to open up to the light and air – and for interiors to connect with the exterior surroundings, and with nature.

Spanning regions and continents as unique as they are diverse, while embracing cultures and languages by the multitude, the tropics lie in a world of vibrant contrast. Where one dominion

In the shade of a breezeway, organic form belies a bench hewn from golden teak, designed by Kanika R'Kul.

Rooms extend seamlessly to the warmth of Sydney's subtropical surroundings, designed by X-Squared.

bears no resemblance to the next, and climates can switch in a moment, from the dazzling to the extreme. There is the perfect realm of ecological wonder where we bathe in the beauty of an archipelago, enjoy palm-fringed beaches and the wonder of the rainforest. There is the arid calm of the desert alongside the antithesis of the urban sprawl that makes up some of the world's most chaotic environments. On the map the tropics are marked between the latitudes of 23.5 degrees to the north of the equator – the Tropic of Cancer – and 23.5 degrees to the south – the Tropic of

Capricorn. In terms of definition, they are, quite simply, worlds apart from anywhere else.

Renowned for his work that translates from the sensual ways of Brazil into the smooth contours of modern architecture and design, the celebrated architect Oscar Niemeyer said, 'It benefits us all to understand a cultural environment to embody a very distinctive sense of place.'

In the tropics, where life spills over quite simply and naturally to the outdoors; the architecture

A bold graphic divide separates a terrace from the entrance, designed by Isay Weinfeld.

The age-old principles of tropical design lie in concepts that have adapted to the elements in the most natural way. They have their roots in the traditions and cultures of warm indigenous styles, and are designed to make a minimal impact on the environment. The Polynesian *bures* and the bungalows of India, for example, make the best use of natural materials that are fit to withstand the weather. Carved and crafted from the land, using nothing more than native hardwoods, stone, palm thatch and bamboo, they provide the perfect living frame for a relaxed lifestyle.

Today, our ecological ways and expanding economies have made this traditional way of life the one we are most likely to visit in the spirit of a holiday. The age-old tropical design concepts carry on in an essential way, such as high ceilings to allow the air to rise and circulate and louvered openings that create natural cross-ventilation, help to catch a cooling breeze and also seal out the extremes of the driving rains and winds of the monsoon. Outside, low roof over-hangs, deep enough to form whole outdoor rooms in the shade, provide the perfect relief from the heat.

corresponds appropriately to the unique surroundings. It is about a design response that caters to a particular way of life and shelters from the elements. There is a need to keep out the sun's harmful rays, the rain and the wind but at the same time a need to let in the breeze and provide plenty of shade. And there is a necessity to reduce the heat and humidity as much as possible by natural means when there is no help from the artificial air-conditioning system to provide relief from the heat.

When life carries out in a breezy, relaxed scene, eating and conversing in the shade of a terrace, there is a sense of completeness felt when there is scarcely any barrier between nature and our own private space. The Malaysian weekend retreat

Absorbing its natural ambience, the layering of cedar forms a gentle transition from the sharp Sydney sunlight to a cool interior, designed by Graham Jahn.

The concept of minimalism – the purity of space that comes from the smooth detailing of linear form and function – corresponds to our surroundings and to a whole tradition, encompassing the design of the home, that turns on an essential way of living. While it stretches across cultures in an eloquent style, the inspiration for minimalism is drawn across time through the simplified and calming ways of the Shaker and the Modernist movements, the monastic order and, naturally, from the Orient. For centuries, the Chinese and Japanese, with their emphasis on living in purist surroundings, have used the concept of *ma*, or the space and balance between objects, and the philosophies of Zen Buddhism – now widely diffused across the globe through the basic principles of design and architecture.

pictured here, by architect Ng Sek San, is a case in point, almost hidden amidst the incredible steamy rainforest that grows wild around it. In a way that lightly touches the land and in a style as inspirational as it is timeless, the simply detailed framework and furnishings are designed to embrace an almost meditative experience of living in harmony with the surrounds. Here, in a place that brings together the most basic of essentials to work a sense of magic, nature can be felt through the clarity of minimalism.

As we seek inspiration in the design, in the style and the mood of our interiors, there is often a defining method that will prove its success. Like the Singapore home shown here, designed by Chan Soo Khian, a result of the owner's wish to live freely in a clear, uninterrupted space. In creating a seamless spatial order throughout, the essentials of comfort and function are perfectly integrated down to the detailed refinement of minimalism, down to the way in which the light shimmers from the reflective pool in the living room, as luxuriously and clearly as Zen calm itself.

Streamlining space with the fresh sensibilities of minimalism fine-tunes the resolve to impose order and eliminate clutter. It provides the perfect background to the increasing day-to-day demands that are made of us, at the same time enhancing the clarity and beauty of our surrounds. As it makes the most of technology and tradition, minimalism embraces the entire spectrum of materials and instils a balance between form, function and spatial order.

As we design, discover and rediscover, opening up the home to embrace the environment is nothing new. In the early twentieth century, legendary Swiss architect Le Corbusier realized a vision of rational ways in which to simplify and refine when building his clean-lined 'machines for living in'. He was creating a new aesthetic in purism that paved the way for the groundbreaking International Style of the time. Sleek and sophisticated, interiors were stripped back from their turn-of-the-century ostentation in response to the new social demands. Even earlier, in 1908, Viennese architect Adolf Loos declared, 'Cultural evolution is equivalent to the removal of ornament'.

Among the handful of designing pioneers that helped forge the way to modernism, the celebrated Sri Lankan architect Geoffrey Bawa's 'cool pleasure pavilions' crossed Asia in perfect harmony with the elements. Others, such as American émigré Ludwig Mies van der Rohe (who coined the term 'less is more') were just as intent on further opening their smooth open-plan interiors to let in the light and the breeze. The streamlining of the low-set Case Study houses located in the warmth of the Californian sun provided indoor-outdoor living with an appeal for lounging around the landscaped edges of swimming pools – examples of these

The cool elegance of natural limestone and cedar-battened screening form an entrance, designed by Stephen Collins, that leads out to a reflecting pool and beautiful garden surrounds.

are vividly captured in the 1960s 'splash' paintings by British artist David Hockney.

While year-round warmth nurtures the desire to surround ourselves with nothing but the bare essentials, there is also a need for peace as we seek time out from it all. Minimalism produces a feeling of pervasive calm, and it is also about opening our senses to the lucid, calming ways of nature. By the water, on the land or in the city, there is an ingenuity that comes with discovering the territory in which we find ourselves, as the following pages show through interiors and exteriors that embrace design in fresh, innovative ways. Here are places that figure strongly in our collective consciousness, where homes capture the essence of summer, of a landscape and a real understanding of how we live. It is an inspirational journey to a place in the sun.

below left + below right
Like sundials, the stark shadows cast from louvres create striking effects while filtering out the sunlight and sea breezes of this waterside haven, designed by Warren & Mahoney.

opposite
The colours of the surrounding sycamore woodlands inspired the subtle hues of this sun-drenched Los Angeles hideaway designed by Koning and Eizenberg.

living
fusing exotic
with modern

In balmy natural surroundings, there is a fresh take on the interior that captures the magic of living. It is sophisticated but down to earth at the same time, naturally free from any visual distraction in order to focus on living as closely as possible to the natural world. The right balance of essentials in the space in which we lounge, listen, watch or work, is all we need to ensure the comfort and respite we seek from the pressures of the day.

It is in the atmosphere of the living room that we take time and care to express our personal style. Here we set the mood for the greater scheme of living that welcomes the flow of activity as we extend warmth and hospitality to family and friends. We can sometimes feel a sense of connection from the outdoor room that is simply screened from the elements or the refinement that comes with the streamlining of sensuous natural materials. As the spaces on the following pages show, the best results are defined in essential simplicity.

Where an interior loosens up and opens out to the sky and the air, its success can lie in how it liaises with the natural beauty of the surroundings. Arranging the living space to make the best use of light and materials in the most integral way can amplify the experience. Immersed in the sights and sounds of Rio de Janeiro's Northern Pantanal wilderness, the retreat designed by Marcio Kogan gives the sensation of living almost at one with nature. With a refined approach that combines native woods with a splash of rich colour within

When our surroundings are as breathtaking as these, the success of a living space is often simply down to its capacity to reflect them.

a seamless spatial order, this interior provides all the comfort that's needed through an essentially minimalist design.

According to master minimalist architect John Pawson, it's not just about white walls and stone floors: 'People tend to focus on the idea of the removal, that it is all somehow a case of throwing out the furniture and painting the walls white. The serious thought that underlies the endeavour is missed. However, real comfort is not about a large sofa either – in my view, many things that look as though they should be comfortable aren't at all. For me comfort is synonymous with a state of total clarity where the eye, the mind and the physical body are at ease, where nothing jars or distracts.'

By employing like-minded materials throughout, storage can be effectively designed to encourage a sense of order. From the flooring to walls lined with built-in storage, shelving or nothing at all, the intrinsic beauty of natural materials brings a tactile refinement to effortlessly even looks that range from the pristine to the rustic. It is here that the consistency of a good design ethos benefits from the smallest detailing to the decor, and it begins with the basis of architectural simplicity.

The spatial qualities of an interior may not be the first thing we notice when we enter a room, as the editor of Australian *Vogue Living* magazine, David

above
In the tropics, interiors designed by Lindsay and Kerry Claire are formed with no walls at all but are separated by finely screened divides and the foliage of the lush Queensland hinterland.

opposite
Hand-hewn stone provides a naturally cool backdrop to the simple but elegant canvas-and-cane furnishings in this Brazilian jungle retreat designed by Marcio Kogan. Scarlet flowers provide a counter-balancing element of colour.

Clark explains: 'Our eye may go to an object or a view, or notice the furniture and decoration. But at the same time that this happens we are also registering (almost subliminally, I believe) the quality of the space we have entered – its proportions and volume, the play of natural light, the materials and finishes, and the connections with the outdoors.'

When an open plan arrangement makes sense, there are numerous elements to take into account within the scheme of everyday living: how we integrate style with function in the kitchen, the dining area, or in both, how we mix the finishes with the furnishings and the decor, and how to unify it all. More importantly, how to simplify it. In the Sydney home designed by Stephen Collins, stone and cedar are juxtaposed in an even style throughout to provide the absolute background for living. In the simple configuration that combines the kitchen, furnishings have been carefully introduced with a keen eye for mixing the elegant simplicity of Asian style with contemporary trends.

There is more to minimalism than simply editing down the excess of things that tend to pile up. Paring down space works because it replaces chaos with calm so, with a lack of complication, comes the freedom of space. Yet designing with the minimalist approach, as some are led to believe, is neither about self-denial, nor the reduction of furniture or ornament. Rather, it's a gentle approach that seeks to minimize clutter, allowing us to focus on the elements that really count. As the celebrated Brazilian architect, Isay Weinfeld said, 'Life's greatest luxury is simplicity.'

A multitude of elements combines in the mix of a great living space. The sense of a truly special place, however, is one that follows the style of a particular life rather than a particular fashion. The following pages capture sensational qualities of interior design, each home conveying its own unique sense of place.

minimal cool

Pristine chic with a distinctly Japanese bent pervades this Singapore oasis designed by Soo Chan of SCDA. The pure, streamlined forms, the delicate hues of the raw silk that cushions the low-level seating, the contrast of gleaming stone with the planar forms of darkly exotic, recycled chengal, and the way in which light reflects from the pool of water beneath the stairs, all combine effortlessly to exude Zen calm.

a room to relax in

In the true essence of tropical living, comfort requires little more than the essentials. Here a solitary armchair invites its owner to sit back and enjoy the view.

the beauty of natural materials

Function lies in the form of a low-slung bench made from honed natural stone. The elegant bust and the bold vase add interest to its sleek shape.

transitional light-to-shade

This restful and uncomplicated room provides a cool, calm haven from the intense light of the exterior, a refuge in which to take some gentle time out when necessary.

lightly veiled *opposite*

Light, gossamer curtains billow in the living room of Brazilian wedding dress designer Marie Toscano, designed by Isay Weinfeld. In a corner furnished with elegant vintage pieces from iconic design duo Carlos Millan and Miguel Forte, the combined simplicity of natural materials creates some interesting ethereal effects. The dressmaker's model adds a quirky, yet totally appropriate touch and the foliage contributes to the overall feeling of airiness.

light elevation

The heat and laser-like light of Bangkok are filtered through this leafy refuge designed by Duanagrit Bunnag; its luminous rooms of white that are sheltered yet open also give rise to outdoor spaces on the upper level while a luscious garden perimeter cushions the hectic inner-city blare.

natural form

A natural spot for contemplation, or a quiet
moment reading alone, extends from the main
bedroom of the Bangkok house featured on the
preceding pages and is outlined with a trellis
and decking made from local red ironwood.

open house *above and opposite*

Where open space has its place, outdoor privacy
in an urban dwelling becomes paramount. Here the
inner walls of a courtyard house designed by Duanagrit
Bunnag define the tropical outdoor sanctum; with floors
of cool limestone that run from inside to out, a dramatic
staircase of cherry wood creates a striking sculptural
element as towering panels of glass accentuate the
openness, folding back to connect with the garden
and a serenely simple setting. The foliage reinforces
the tranquillity of the space, as well as suggesting
a feeling of coolness and calm.

organic screen

In this cool and pared-back decor designed
by Singapore-based SCDA the eye focuses on
the leafy background, which fully captures the
exotic allure of the tropics. A light and delicate
transparent curtain forms a screening wall
that provides privacy.

laid-back elegance *opposite*

On the western shores of Florida, a serene
setting designed by Toshiko Mori captures the
casual ease of its small barrier island surrounds.
In wide-open spaces that are furnished with a
uniquely stylized collection, a Philippe Starck
chaise longue adds a sensual ripple to tropical
beachside vacationing.

serene style *top right and right*

According to Brazilian architect Isay Weinfeld,
the greatest luxury of all is simplicity. Seemingly
worlds apart from the urban grit and grind of
São Paulo, living rooms that extend to pools and
palm trees also rely on the right choice of decor
for their resolute sense of calm: the lacquered
patina of a nineteenth-century Chinese table
and smooth lounge chairs from the modernist
greats. Inherited or collected, these pieces are
carefully blended with the upbeat simplicity
of Brazilian chic.

panorama

Immersed in the canopies of Rio de Janeiro's Northern Pantanal, a weekend retreat designed by Marcio Kogan combines the warmth of exotic woods and a richly toned mix of decor in true Carioca style. With an expansive sweep of picture windows to embrace the jungle environment, this interior is designed for the cooler of tropical climes where temperatures often drop to zero after the heavy haze of the sun sets over the hills. The overhead paper lampshades are both functional and fun.

living colour

To punctuate a mood with colour, beautiful and eye-catching furniture in saturated shades and deep hues such as these lounge chairs, by designers Pierre Paulin [above] and Christian Werner [opposite] play a key role within their otherwise neutrally toned schemes.

LA cool *below*

Loft-style living is entirely suited to hot climates. With flexible partitions and enough glass to allow light to flood right through, this Los Angeles home designed by architect Stephen Ehrlich is the perfect example.

tactile warmth *right*

Casual living unfolds to the outdoors in a sensually textured room, designed by Jon King, of roughly hewn basalt stone, dark timber beams and richly upholstered furnishings.

elemental elegance *opposite*

'It's about striking a balance with nature,' says designer Ng Sek San of his rain forest realm located north of Kuala Lumpur. Swathed in an atmosphere as dramatic as it is natural, the same simple gestures in the elemental materials and decor apply to both the interior and the exterior.

sinuous form *above*

To celebrate one element is to balance another. The gnarled shape of the tree trunk and branches in this picture echoes the smooth curve of the unusual lounger in the foreground. Both complement each other beautifully and fuse to create an elegant, harmonious whole.

natural layering *page 40*

On the edge of Brazil's Atlantic Rainforest, layers of bamboo, hand-hewn arenite stone and wicker furnishings form the laid-back appeal that's perfect for a low-maintenance holiday hideaway, designed by Marcio Kogan.

smooth contrast *page 41*

Like yin and yang, an ambient harmony belies a smooth mix of B&B Italia sofas and classic Charles and Ray Eames chairs with an Oriental spice in a room of warm teak floors designed by Singapore-based WoHa.

textural mix *opposite*

A raffia-papered sliding screen and a roughly hewn wall of basalt stone imbue this interior, designed by Stephen Collins, with tactile warmth. The red of the upholstery and the glass vase add further richness and depth.

linear rule *above*

The strong horizontal lines of the limestone floors, seamless glazing and a western red cedar-battened ceiling provide the basis to relaxed Sydney living in a distinctively timeless and elegant style. Designed by Stephen Collins.

cascading design

The soothing sound of water forms a tranquil ambience within the textural warmth

of this interior, designed by Singapore-based SCDA. Calming neutral colours emphasize

this tranquillity, while the red leather armchair and footstool make a bold statement.

making an entrance *above*

This spacious and elegantly streamlined entrance lined in western red cedar and punctuated by carefully arranged plants, is both warm and welcoming. When closed, the glass panels accentuate the horizontal lines of the interior. Designed by Stephen Kidd.

transitional space *opposite*

A transitional corner provides a quiet and intimate place in which to relax. Transitional spaces such as this need not be wasted. With a bit of thought they can be put to functional use, as well as adding extra interest. Designed by Louise Nettleton.

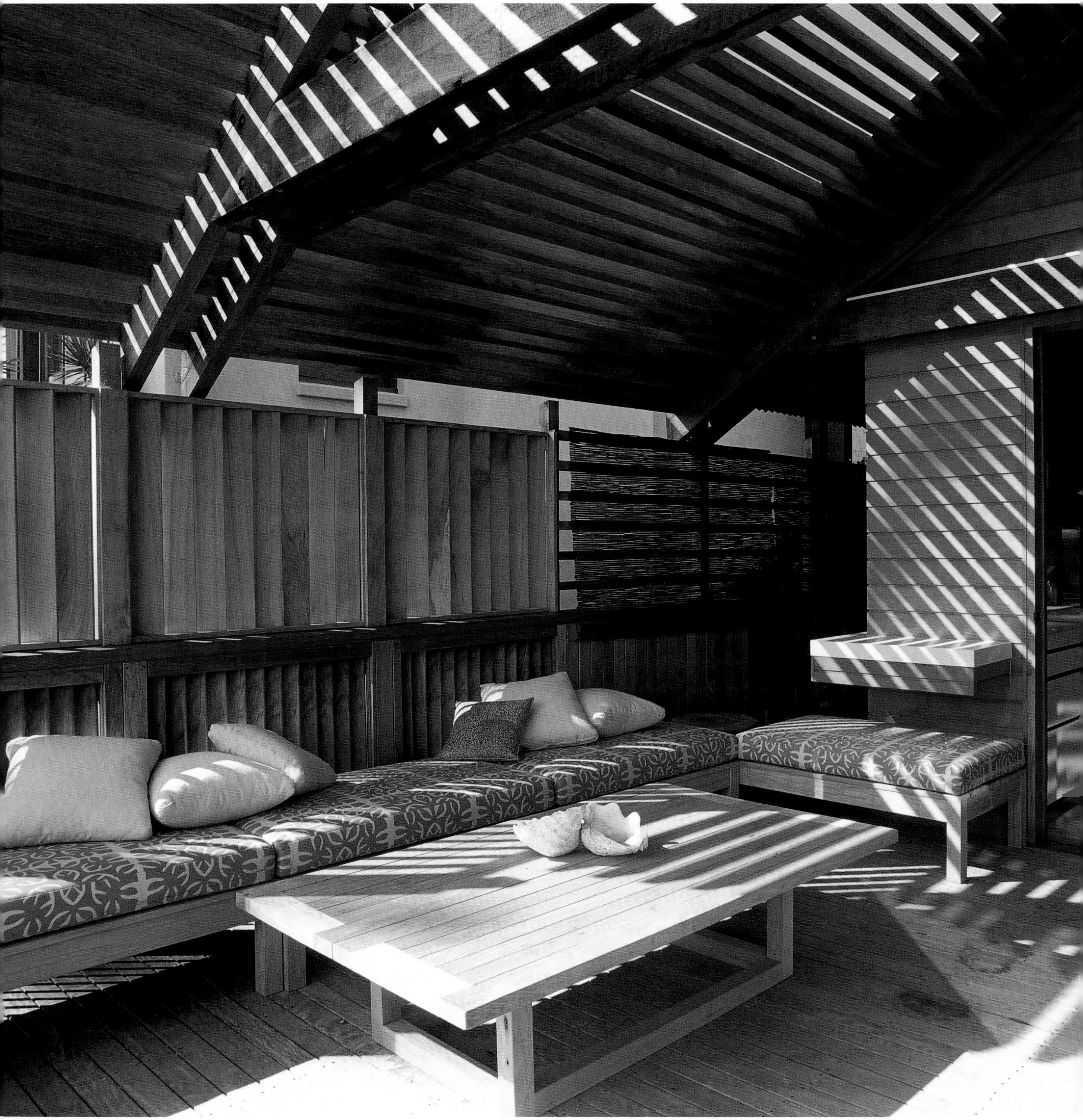

into the shade *page 48*

Creating an environment in which to relax and soak up the warmth is second nature to the Sydney firmament of indoor-outdoor living. Here, beneath the shade of a timber pergola, laid-back living spills out from the interior, designed by Graham Jahn.

light well *page 49*

A picture window lets in the light as well as providing a scenic outlook in this transitional space designed by Graham Jahn. Cleverly arranged sculpture adds style and interest.

in the mesh *left*

Sliding doors of stainless-steel mesh, designed by Singapore-based WoHa, create a filter to soften the light as well as to screen out insects in a solution that is both attractive and functional at the same time.

catching the breeze *opposite*

Designed by Lindsay and Kerry Claire to catch any zephyr of a cooling breeze, louvred walls of glass naturally cross-ventilate, eliminating the need for air conditioning in this living space that features tallow-wood flooring and classic 1960s woven cane chairs by Danish designer Poul Kjaerholm.

cooking and dining
celebrating good tastes

Everything goes on in the kitchen. The most dynamic zone in the home is the ongoing place to indulge, refuel and sustain. While cooking, eating and drinking take up the main focus, the kitchen nurtures as much our emotional well-being, bringing family and friends together to the table both indoors and out. It's a place of ritual and routine, and we gravitate towards it, not only when appetites are at their keenest, but to carry out any number of movements at any time of the day. Where functional simplicity comes into play, the essentials are streamlined with the use of natural materials and extend to make the most of our surroundings.

As the heart and life of the interior opens up and merges with the outdoors, the essential design of the kitchen needs to be seamless. Where the pleasures of food and all of its creative pursuits take place, the focus is on ways to ensure the simplest of functional solutions, in the best possible light. From preparation to celebration, the kitchen embraces a whole profusion of activities right down to the equipment we choose and how we use it, so everything here needs to be thought through in the best possible way and tailored to fit in comfortably with our lifestyle. Most probably we will not sit back and enjoy it all as often as we would like. While we search

for time out from our schedule we find ourselves eating to live on the run, rather than living to eat – and relaxing. To function smoothly, a kitchen, whether it serves the purpose of snacking or feasting, needs to perform like a sleek, well-oiled machine. From finding the correct balance to fine-tuning, establishing an efficient space starts with determining how we want our kitchen to operate at different times of the day. The ins and outs of everyday routines and requirements need to figure into user-friendly functionalism, taking place in a space that can seamlessly and repeatedly reinvent itself.

To maximize the concept of open plan, integrating the kitchen and dining areas into a complete living zone basically relies on carrying through the same or like-minded surface finishes, task and ambient lighting, wall and floor treatments and furnishings. This consistency ensures cohesion and continuity. From work surfaces to the joinery, whether it's the stripped-back industrial aesthetic of exposed, raw concrete finishes, as in the Bangkok kitchen shown, choosing the right materials will help create the right ambience and at the same time bring a space to life.

In selecting the best combinations you have to take into account wear-and-tear factors but also consider how successfully materials will weather the environment. Natural materials exude tactile warmth and elegance, from the sensual tones of wood to the honed beauty of stone; marine-quality stainless steel withstands the corrosion of sea air, while the persevering durability of concrete, ceramics, quartz composites and laminate, rubber or resin all provide perfect combinations – the choices are endless.

below and opposite

Located as far south as Omaha beach on the subtropical west coast of New Zealand, function meets form in a modular setting designed by Fearon Hay that flows on to a private pool court.

In the kitchen designed by Graham Jahn, the softened tones of cedar panelling, stone work surfaces and colour-backed glass in vivid green all combine seamlessly to reflect the native beauty of the Sydney Harbour foreshore. Here creating somewhere to relax and take in the warmth is second nature to the relaxed, indoor-outdoor way of living. Using the same evenness in the streamlining of materials through the kitchen to the dining and living area, it all unfolds on to a deep-shaded terrace, where spectacular views across delicately silvered water and a curve of white sand just below complete the picture.

Where the climate beckons to the barbecue and a table close by, it's simply a matter of creating an easy access from the kitchen as we decamp to the veranda, the garden or the terrace. In the Malaysian rainforest retreat of Ng Sek San, like a transparent tree house, much of weekend life is taken up outdoors on the deck. This includes the cooking and eating that are carried out with an innovative, if not entirely laid-back, approach to the kitchen. With nothing but a giant traditional *kuali* wok that takes the form of a barbecue, it doubles up as the hearth for the fire and the grill. Like the reclaimed industrial grating that forms the table, it is an appropriate, minimal, low-energy and environmentally friendly approach to cooking in the tropics.

In more usual circumstances, there is a logical solution to excess heat in the kitchen with the addition of the extended 'wet' kitchen. From Asia to South America the traditional, naturally ventilated semi-outdoor space – once made with walls of slatted bamboo or rattan – is equipped to wok-fry or slow-cook and designed to keep the internal kitchen labour-saving clean, cool and fume-free for food preparation and casual meals.

Keep cooking and eating areas streamlined and uncluttered, for maximum efficiency and ease of use.

The key to a good working kitchen lies within a design that incorporates effective storage. Basically considered as one extensive storage solution (yet there can never be enough), concealed or on show, there needs to be a defining order that will take into account everything from the utensils to the build-up of appliances and keeping wine where it's supposed to be, in a cool dark place. The resolve to store is best worked out by means of smooth functional simplicity. Where integrating the functions can sometimes be hard to achieve, the practical options of an island bench, a generous walk-in larder or a flush line-up of built-in cupboards

can open out and maximize space. Effective streamlining frees up space on the work surfaces and allows us to get on and enjoy time spent in a perfectly planned haven.

In a home on the shores of the Gulf of Mexico, everything is streamlined to focus on the spectacular sea outlook. The dining space, designed by Toshiko Mori with the pared-back simplicity of minimalism, provides the immaculate setting from where to sit back and take it all in. As this chapter shows, defining the essential elements is all that's needed to focus on enhancing the way we live.

natural contour *above*

The tapering curve of a silver ash table, designed by Caroline Casey, a sleek counter of pressed stainless steel and a suspended Aboriginal fishing trap lead the eye to sweeping views of Pittwater Bay in this naturally refined dining kitchen designed by Sydney-based Dawson Brown.

solar dining *opposite*

In an open space full of light, sky and water this dining scene hovers over the edge of the Gulf of Mexico. This interior is idyllic in its simplicity, but, since the weather in this part of the world can be as unpredictable as it is torrid, Toshiko Mori has designed it to contend with hurricanes, corrosive salt and harsh light, thus creating a fortress of quiet strength.

shutter setting *opposite*

With folding shutters to filter out sea breezes
and sunlight, there's nothing more pleasurable
than sitting back in the cool of this deep-set
veranda designed by Susan Reed, to indulge
in the delights of a long leisurely lunch in
Byron Bay.

cool dining *above*

This dining area in São Paulo, designed by Isay
Weinfeld, connects directly and seamlessly to
an outdoor haven.

centrepiece *right*

In the true style of courtyard-house living,
rooms unfold one into another between inside
and out, and in every aspect are bound with light.
Comprising a sleek line-up of retractable units and
a stainless-steel island that spans the far wall, this
room is centred largely on the table of activities,
designed by Duanagrit Bunnag.

shades of white *page 64, bottom right + page 65*

White in the kitchen suggests overtones of
cleanliness, purity and freshness, and surfaces
of stainless steel and polished concrete form a
space that is functional, practical and appropriate.
Designed by Alex Smith of Sydney-based CSA
Architects. Adding further to the purist's touch
is a set of 'Series 7' chairs by Arne Jacobsen.

functional viewing *page 64, top*
An otherwise purely functional space
is designed so as not to distract from
the fabulous view. The subdued hues
of honed granite, stainless steel and
enamel-backed glass contribute to
an overall effect of uncomplicated
smoothness. Designed by Toshiko Mori.

steeling beauty *page 64, bottom left*
Drawing from the rich tones of native
brush box floorboards, the warmth
of this Queensland beachside kitchen
serves up an exotic flavour. Designed by
Warren Naylor to conceal a preparation
area and appliances, the retractable wall
becomes a seamless feature alongside
its compact stainless-steel counterpart.

open plan *above and opposite*
With smooth, natural materials that
integrate effortlessly between the
kitchen and living areas, rooms open up
to breathe and focus on enhancing the
way we live rather than containing it.

tonal ingredient

In all its sensual elegance, walnut veneer combines with stainless steel to create an open, functional kitchen, designed by Rod Radziner, that oozes textural warmth and style.

in the hot seat

Transferring the cool refinement of the interior to the terrace, a sleek hearth made from stainless steel and concrete delivers a dose of fireside warmth that is conducive to evening entertaining. Designed by Simon Carnachan.

eating out *opposite*

Sunlight filters through the trees to a warm LA terrace setting in which the deep charcoal-grey fire-surround blends to match the sleek outdoor table and chairs that have also been designed by Ron Radziner.

jungle kitchen

Here an entirely laid-back approach emerges from the rainforest canopies of Serendah. In an open sky and an environment that's harsh and consuming, this exterior provides a giant *kuali*, the traditional wok, and industrial grating for a low table, while mats made from rattan and tree bark soften the utilitarian interior. Designed by Ng Sek San, this is an appropriate, low-energy and environmentally sympathetic way to a weekend escape.

integral cool

Just like the naturally shaded cool of the
surrounding wilderness, this retreat,
designed by Marcio Kogan, mixes refinement
with functionality.

tapered effect *opposite*
Overlooking Queensland's Sunshine Beach, this kitchen space is angled along a living area to capture the vast Pacific Ocean views. Designed by Brisbane-based John Mainwaring.

pavilion splendour *above*
You can almost feel the breeze off Sydney Harbour through the pavilion designed by Graham Jahn. Bound by wide openings at either end, its striking cathedral ceiling embraces the combined living, dining and kitchen space in beautiful cedar detailing, in which the principles of integral, natural materials and coolly stylish furnishings, such as the Frank O. Gehry 'Powerplay' chairs apply.

natural cohesion *overleaf*
Evoking the native beauty from around the Sydney Harbour foreshore, the soothing tones of timber, vivid green and charcoal grey reflect the colours of tree ferns and sandstone crags in this kitchen that unfolds to the open living space, a deeply shaded terrace and the beach below. Designed by Graham Jahn.

industrial strength *left*

The stripped-down industrial aesthetic of exposed ductwork, raw concrete finishes and black-framed furniture by Mario Botta in an open kitchen that sits quietly insulated in a verdant tangle of foliage. Spacious and airy, this space is ideal for relaxed, informal entertaining. Designed by Prabhakorn Vadanyakul.

luminous attraction *above*

Beneath the firefly-glow of light, a deep orange colour beams from a set of 1970s Enzo Mari 'Box' chairs and reflects from the Perspex-topped dining table, creating a feeling of warmth and conviviality. Designed by Andrew Lister.

sleeping and relaxing
giving in to the elements

We enter the private world of the bedroom to seek refuge, in an environment where we can be at peace, silent and still. It is here where we begin and end the day – winding down to switch off from the rest of the world – rejoicing in the calm of our innermost thoughts and dreams. Minimalism seeks to refine space and materials to their purist form. It manifests itself in the textures and tones of natural materials, in the way in which the play of light is diffused over surfaces and, in the bedroom, in the overall ambience. Appealing to all the senses in the most fundamental way, in splendid isolation, the bedroom is the perfect space for restoring the soul.

This is the room in which we spend a third of our lives and we call for familiar notions of comfort in an environment that lets us feel entirely at peace – in contemplation, meditation and sleep. Here, with little or no distractions but the surrounding luscious visuals, we can cocoon ourselves in the calm of the sleeping zone. The effects of minimalism, as it seeks to refine the balance and harmony of space, work instinctively in the bedroom, because taking the first step towards transcendence begins when a space feels essentially right to all the senses.

More so than in any other room of the interior, it is in the bedroom where we need to resolve the visual chaos of the day by means of a calming sense of order. An example in point is the realm of peace designed by SCDA in the Japanese vein of minimalist simplicity, not only through the meticulous attention to detail but with the inspiring ingenuity that lies in its seamless open plan. As space flows freely between the functional essentials of sleeping, storing, and the en-suite, there is an effortless cohesion of materials, while the mood takes to meditative in light-filled purity.

The simple pleasures to be enjoyed in a light-filled room are when warmth, ambience and textural diversity come to life through clear definition. For some the bedroom can also be the perfect place to occupy during the day as well. Given enough floor space, when the right proportions allow, the bedroom can extend to comprise the luxury of a personal living room, a retreat for reading or perhaps a quiet corner devoted to a study space when we really need to get away it all.

Best described as the 'unfilled' room of the interior, the editor of Australian lifestyle magazine *Inside Out*, Karen McCartney explains: 'When a room is very sparely furnished the decorative elements become highly significant. A chair, an ottoman, or stool must not only be appropriate, but inspiring in their simplicity and placement. Tonally and texturally, furniture can either complement the overall design of the room or add a note of pleasing contrast.'

In an ideal world we would have our clothes arranged in a room of their own. If this is not an option, however, then there are plenty of other ideas to help you overcome the usual compromising of floor space with the wardrobe in the bedroom. Keeping clean simple lines free from the bulk of freestanding units needs clever devising and designing with smart, inbuilt sensitivity, such as transforming the bedhead into a partitioning storage wall that can work

to accommodate a great deal of wardrobe-storing solutions.

To open up our space to the light and follow the path of the sun, catching the first rays of sunrise invites a quiet, aesthetic contemplation in which to begin the day. As the age-old theory prescribes: orientating the bedroom and our bed towards the east will attune our bodies to the cycle of light, and thus make us more likely to awake clear-

Japanese-inspired sensibilities are a source of calming coolness in this bedroom designed by Singapore-based SCDA.

minded and refreshed. Where the sun shines very brightly, however, there is a need to diffuse the intensity of its rays and screen them out in the bedroom.

There are many different ways to keep the sun at bay at different times of the day without having to resort to conventional curtains. The huge resource of louvres, screens and sliding walls, such as those shown from Australia to Brazil made of beautiful timber lattice, can either bring a warm textural aesthetic as a design feature to the room or can be integrated within the framing of the window. This allows us to control the light, to throw the room open to the view at sunrise or to close it down to a dark and restful enclosure. Just as vitally important is the circulation of cool fresh air.

Pale wood panelling makes an elegant spatial divide between wardrobe and bedroom. Designed by Toshiko Mori.

In the bedroom calming influences from natural daylight to a nocturnal glow are as essential as deep shadow and darkness. Candles have a remarkable effect that encourages rest in hypnotic ways, and can be just as pleasing to the eye when used at the same time as the lights are dimmed low. As sleep is associated with purity, it's only natural that the qualities of a soothing colour palette should reside in the bedroom. Here, the opportunity for a magical approach to lighting is defined in our affinity with the surrounds.

The following rooms are arranged for peace and silence, and lend themselves to clear and intimate visuals of nature. In even the remotest of retreats there remains a need to create the ultimate personal sleeping refuge. In hot climates taking time out to contemplate and reflect requires a cooling space – from amid an almost-bare exposure to the verdant Malaysian jungle canopy from the confines of a hammock, or ensconced on a daybed beneath the soothing sounds of rainfall on glass. Whichever the solution, the mood induces a pervasive calm, for it is only at peace that we can sleep.

brilliant awakening

As the first rays of sunlight stream into this
bedroom that faces due east over the Pacific,
they are absorbed by the soft textural tones of the
walls and decor. Sliding panels within a folding
screen help to darken what would otherwise be
a very bright and early awakening. Designed by
John Mainwaring.

screening technique *opposite*

This elegant and unusual headboard, which doubles up as the partitioning screen to the living area, was once a set of elevator doors. Designed by Brisbane-based Bloc Design.

daydream *above*

Flanked by towering bamboo, an integral daybed is given an exotic edge in the northern New South Wales hinterland. Designed by Elizabeth Watson Brown.

tropical calm

A place for everything, and everything in its place.
Plenty of integrated storage is concealed behind
this tall headboard while a timber-veneered recess
replaces the need for bedside table in a room that
slides right back to a tropical canvas of green.
Designed by Elizabeth Watson Brown.

inclined to relax *page 92*

A coolly padded corner provides a framed view
and welcome respite from the swelter of the
Queensland bushland. Designed by Brisbane-based
Bloc Design.

comfort zone *page 93*

Embellished by sensual colours and textures,
this haven designed by Giovanni D'Ercole opens
out to the living space, sea breezes and a magnetic
view to the Pacific.

screen divide *above*

A folding timber screen designed by Marcio Kogan provides a tactile divide between this spacious, airy bedroom and its jungle surroundings.

chilled out *opposite*

Lattice screens filter the light and encase the cool within a simple room of stone walls and pebble-set flooring, designed by Marcio Kogan.

open style *page 96*

Like its cedar-screened exterior, the flexible space of this interior, designed by Graham Jahn, unfolds and changes according to the owner's shifting needs.

zone out *page 97*

The calming solitude of nature prevails beneath the exposed elements of a slumber zone, designed by Prabhakorn Vadanyakul.

jungle wrap *left*

Like cradles swinging among the canopies,
generously proportioned canvas hammocks
induce the correct mood for meditation and
relaxation within the heady surrounds of architect
Ng Sek San's weekend rainforest hideaway.

transparent repose *above*

Prabhakorn Vadanyakul has created an exclusive
spot in which to settle back in comfort on a Mies
van der Rohe daybed and peer lazily through the
glass at the thundering rains of the monsoon.

slumberland *opposite*

Breathing in the heady scents of the surrounding forest of eucalyptus
is a natural sedative in the Queensland hinterland, designed by Lindsay
and Kerry Claire.

warm seclusion *above left*

The sensual hues of walnut panelling in this simple and restful bedroom
designed by Ron Radziner are chosen to complement the deep greens of
the surrounding treetops while opening to reveal ideal nooks for storage.

integral divide *above right*

In this bedroom, designed by Tim Roberts, a low-rise headboard frees up
space and provides a clever opening to the outdoors. A straightforward
angle-poise lamp on the floor facilitates bedtime reading with the
minimum of visual fuss.

seductive retreat

Luxury and light are the keynotes of this five-star
hotel room designed by Singapore-based SCDA.
Cool, clear lines and furniture designed by
Minotti complete the comfort experience.

bathing
the quest for freshness

Where it's hot, the need to feel refreshed is absolute. In the tropics, essential bathing rituals take place within the splendid isolation of a naturally minimalist environment, when all we need are the soothing sounds of water flowing in the simplest of surroundings – whether a space of pure white-on-white, or the sensual, contemplative tones of natural materials. As stress is replaced with serenity and chaos with calm, the bathing area goes beyond the functional and the routine: it's about taking care of both body and soul in the natural world.

The most compact room of the interior, this is a small space made large. As the bathing area has moved beyond its focus on functionality to one of sensuality, it has become a sought-after sanctum, a tranquil retreat from the stresses of everyday living. We expect a fast and effective way of getting clean with the feel-good factor at the turn of a tap; an instant reviver thanks to a hard-hitting shower or a long indulgent soak. Bathing is about slowing down in an atmosphere that is conducive to the pursuit of tranquillity.

As with the exhilarating feeling of plunging into the ocean, the elemental pleasures of at-home bathing are infinite. The universal value of water shapes the way, as the bathroom becomes a celebration of the act of bathing. Water, the constant essential, the life source, is also a revered resource and a material to be used sparingly. By clarifying and purifying certain essential features, we can elevate bathing to a sensory experience and eliminate any jarring extravagance that would detract from the pursuit of freshness.

Because we require only a limited range of components to achieve a perfect aesthetic result, the bathing area's physical environment calls for a serious focus on design. In every aspect, from freestanding to wall-mounted fixtures and fittings, ventilation and the invisible network of plumbing and pipes, the bathroom must be durable, reassuring and reliable. Unlike furniture in the living room, which can be moved and re-arranged time and again, nothing is haphazard here. Permanence calls for useful, logical design.

Rectilinear steel on marble in this up-to-the-minute yet timelessly elegant bathroom in São Paulo, designed by Isay Weinfeld.

The Japanese bathhouse, essentially an uninterrupted space with no divides to distract from refining the art of contemplation, has not only been a great source of inspiration but also a great influence. It illustrates clearly how, when there is only a limited amount of space available, the simplest way to enhance it is to have it read as a whole. A single walk-in space where water can drain directly to the floor, it allows natural light and air to flow right through. Streamlined and pared back without the fuss of screens, the wet-room also easily ventilates, which is of paramount importance in the tropical environment.

The closest connections with nature count in the smallest of spaces. As shown here, an awkward space, even without windows, can still be effective. Designed by Prabhakorn Vadanyakul, with nothing but the essentials to let in a flood of daylight from above, the feeling of showering beneath a tropical sky is enhanced by the recessed planting of lush foliage, which also serves the practical purpose of reducing humidity.

This is the age of the designer bathroom, where innovation goes hand in hand with technology, at the same time revitalizing the form and function of the traditional. Water flow makes a feature of aerated spouts, heads and jets that are designed to drench, delivering effects that range from multi-massage to the tropical downpour, all within a hedonistic framework, and all designed increasingly to indulge.

Clean lines and clever detailing reduce visual distraction and ensure sublime experience.

Keeping up with the latest in high-tech bathroom design, however, is not always easy. With the hugely rich variety of elements to enhance our bathing experience that is available today, careful thought has to be given to choosing the right combination of materials, textures, tones and styles in order to create the right look.

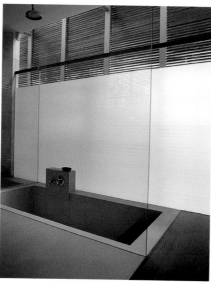

A solid and functional bathroom solution in Queensland, designed by Warren Naylor.

Sinking into a Singapore haven, designed by SCDA.

The angle on glass in Kuala Lumpur, designed by Ngiom.

When all we need is the grace of natural materials around us, the cooling qualities of stone or the rich warmth of hardwoods in the bathroom can instil a unique ambience of comfort and calm. Still, in hot and wet conditions both indoors and out, not all hardwoods are practical, as some remain susceptible to expanding and contracting. Many, on the other hand, such as the widely used teak and Brazilian ipé, weather with wear and improve with age when naturally treated and sealed from the wet, and also tolerate humidity.

Defined by innovative ways that capture the magic of fusing the exterior and the interior, is the bathroom designed by Marcio Kogan. Here the graphic divide of latticed wood acts like a breathing skin between the interior and the lush rainforest surrounds, and there is an added sense of coolness in the shower room that remains shaded when opened out to encourage airflow and provides an intimate connection with the surroundings.

All personal care accessories, including scented candles and the essential oils of aromatherapy, should all be kept out of sight but within easy reach. Storage units, shelving and modular cupboards can be streamlined, or concealed behind flush mirrors and recessed niches. Keeping clutter at bay ensures that your restorative haven remains cool, calm and connected to nature – the best way to engage all the senses as we make our bathing area a sanctuary of tranquillity and freshness.

exotic edge

On the edge of Brazil's Atlantic Rainforest, unfurling
Heliconia provides a sumptuous backdrop to this
shower room lined with milky glass mosaic tiles.
Designed by Marcio Kogan.

elemental divide   *page 112*
Sliding wide open to a lattice
screen of timber, neutral surfaces
of glass mosaic and concrete
add to the cooling ambience in
this shower room designed by
Marcio Kogan.

steam room   *page 113*
In the steamy realms of Bangkok,
lush foliage soaks up the skylight
sunshine in a shower room designed
by Prabhakorn Vadanyakul.

designs on nature   *above left*
Singapore architect Soo Chan's
clean lines have the exotic edge;
with bamboo planted to benefit the
softly filtered daylight, the sensual
darkness of a chengal bench and
flooring add to the feeling of
indulgence.

bold diffusion   *above right*
Rhythmic strokes of light, timber
and frosted glass form a striking
solution to privacy in São Paulo.
Designed by Isay Weinfeld.

integrally reclined   *opposite*
Creating a space that appeals to all
the senses, Kim Jones of Jones and
Sonter designed this Sydney haven
that features plantation-grown
teak, stainless-steel wall panelling
and an innovative approach to
integrating the bathtub. Opening
on to a small deck, a pond and the
garden, the bathing experience is
virtually taken outdoors.

forest cool   *left*

Making the most of the environment, eucalyptus trunks come naturally to hand here. Designed by Brisbane-based Bloc Design, this cooling space in which to bathe is given the shaded treatment. Seamless glass divides integrate the interior into the exterior.

feature contrast   *above*

Embracing colour with glass mosaic tiles, walls extend from the sunken bath to a dramatic glass ceiling. Designed by Andrew Lister.

outdoor elements   *page 118*

In high humidity, where things never seem to dry, an alcove provides the practical basis for bathing al fresco. Designed Ng Sek San.

neutral palette   *page 119*

In neutrally toned seclusion, the tactile feature of river stones and running water provides a contemplative atmosphere for this bathroom designed by Judy Houlton.

exposure *above left*

Native teng wood panels and an open sky provide the perfect outdoor bathing experience in a beachfront retreat on the south coast of Thailand, designed by Kanika R'Kul. The sleek chrome fittings and the elegantly rounded washbasin, which manage to be both functional and sophisticated at the same time, prevent the effect from being too rugged.

functional direction *above right*

The bathroom space here, designed by Ng Sek San, conveniently extends to the outdoors in true utilitarian style, although the large-leaved plant introduces a homely decorative element.

angled view *opposite*

Bold and daringly modern, a Philippe Starck-designed freestanding tub and spout sets the scene in a shady room of soft charcoal walls that connects to secluded spot for drying off in the Queensland sun, designed by John Mainwaring. As well as being convenient, the simple, understated towel rail that runs around the tub also emphasizes the elegant oval shape.

island influence *page 122*

Old Indian temple doors lead the way to a sybaritic retreat designed by Giovanni D'Ercole on the Pacific shores of Byron Bay. Walls of woven bamboo separate the living area, Indonesian Java stone divides

the bathing area, while darkly stained wooden floors add to the harmonious fusion that evokes a feeling of tropical island luxury. Twin square basins add order and symmetry, and the deep shelving arrangement beneath them provides a useful and attractive storage space for towels and similar necessities.

smooth luxury *page 123*

Keeping the focus on natural cool, the refined travertine forms a light-filled bathing haven, designed by Brisbane-based Elizabeth Watson Brown. The smooth lines and tranquil atmosphere make this a peaceful private sanctuary.

cool outlook *left*

Cornered into a limited space, this en suite bathroom maximizes its intake of light and views over the South China Sea through a sliding timber partition in this beachfront weekender, designed by Kanika R'Kul.

shower refinement *above*

Representing the ethos of simplicity, form and function, Graham Jahn combines the qualities of colour-backed glass, teak and marble in a compact and cleverly designed dual shower room that seamlessly connects to the bedroom.

luminosity *opposite*

Bathroom design is expressed in just a few select materials for surfaces and finishes, while the main precept is keeping in touch with light. Here the partitioning is made with the translucency of frosted glass that enables daylight to flood in and suggests a feeling of aquatic coolness. Designed by Singapore-based WoHa.

sybaritic form *above*

In a clean-lined space of ambient calm, the sinuous form of an old-fashioned roll-top bath is positioned to take in the stunning garden view. Designed by Duanagrit Bunnag.

outdoor spaces
rooms beyond rooms

The tropics are about outdoor lifestyle, about dissolving the boundaries between inside and out.

The tropics are a hotbed of botanical exuberance, with their intensity of colour, scent (which is at its most intoxicating at sunset) and sensual surroundings. With the almost-everyday warmth that encourages an outdoor lifestyle, there is every good reason for interior rooms to become part of the garden. With an emphasis on the essential simplicities of minimalism – the pleasing proportions of space, the cohesion of primary materials, and the exclusion of anything superfluous – the outdoors can blend with the interior, with spectacular interpretations.

In essence, the scene is perfect when we step from our private sanctum right into nature – from the shade to the place that enables us to feel in touch with the seasons, the elements, the trees and the rain. The sun shines over these latitudes all through the year, giving the long languid days that are typical of hot-climate living. This lifestyle is governed by a variety of cultural riches but it is, above all, about fresh air living. To make the most

it, there is the idyllic retreat of the outdoor room to provide the ultimate sanctuary, a place where we can be nurtured and where we can breathe.

The design roots of minimalism in the outdoor areas of the home and the garden boast a rich history. They owe an immense debt to the influence drawn from the symbolic gardens of the East, in which balance and harmony became a reverential focus of the interior, and the same ideas of simplicity and formal reduction went into transforming the intermediate exterior. Meditative water and rock compositions and the perfection of raked-gravel courtyards that were nurtured from the fifteenth century continue to inspire design solutions today.

'A perfect garden, no matter what its size is, should enclose nothing less than the entire universe,' as the celebrated master Mexican modernist, Luis Barragán 'said. With his lucid clarity, he translated this notion into

his minimalist interpretations, particularly the vividly coloured walled gardens and courtyards extending out from open-plan interiors. In the same vein, the streamlined outdoor scenes created by legendary Brazilian designer, Roberto Burle Marx were among the great influences of twentieth-century landscape design.

Today, with our focus on ecological awareness, our outdoor areas provide the perfect backdrop for fresh innovative takes on the outdoor room, the courtyard, patio, porch, terrace and veranda in all their variations of environments. Where the

ideal for essential living is to relate and integrate the interior to the outside the emphasis is on creating a cohesive framework to a rich visual source and, more importantly, the sense of belonging to nature.

As the warmth permits us to extend indoor living to the outdoors, the outdoor room is as much a place for defining a mood and a creative expression as the interior is. The design sensibilities of the interior, such as clean simple lines and similar or like-minded materials can thus be extended to the exterior. Floorboards

The shadows cast on Giovanni D'Ercole's Byron Bay sundeck facing the sea produce a mesmerizing effect.

São Paulo's urban context falls away in a corner of lush, open-air privacy. Designed by Isay Weinfeld.

and timber decking, stone and paving are among the most effective ways to link the two smoothly so the house and the outdoor areas can be considered as one.

However, designing space that is exposed to the reality of the elements can sometimes prove to be quite a challenge. Materials age quickly through the year-round harshness of the heat and the humidity, the effects of the monsoon. In spite of the climate and its ravages we make a refuge of the outdoors and embrace the shade, as in the perfect outdoor comfort zone, designed by Soo Chan Khian, in which to shelter from the elements in Singapore. As it catches a refreshing breeze and shades from the sunlight, a rich textural palette forms the simple yet refined backdrop against which to relax by the edge the pool.

In the steaming heat of Bangkok, the necessity to shade the exterior needs year-round attention. The example shown of a private verdant garden that grows wild around the house designed by Prabhakorn Vadanyakul has been densely planted to soften the harsh, reflective surfaces of the mostly-glass exterior. The heavy canopy provides a perfect filter through which to diffuse the sun, at the same time helping to relieve the

If it's not quite hot enough, relax and escape to the sauna. Designed by Sydney-based Tim Roberts.

humidity. Replete with an integral outdoor room that extends to take in the scenic sensations around the swimming pool, it is through essential simplicities that the lush tropical oasis can best be defined.

The pursuit of paradise is nothing new, but we often forget that it can be closer to home than we think. These unique places celebrate the sheer beauty of an uninterrupted wilderness, an oasis that belies the urban sprawl. As all of these spaces show, it is the pure enjoyment of the simpler things that can lure us from the routine to a private vantage point, angled so as to keep an eye on where the sun shines and on how the wind blows. A place in the sun that provides the perfect scene, like nature intended.

colour fusion *opposite*

Taking a cue from the saturated, sunburnt colours of the northern New
South Wales hinterland, this guesthouse designed by Elizabeth Watson-
Brown nestles into beautiful surroundings and offers shelter and shade.

Pacific luxury *above*

A stunning view, perfect weather and a pristine pool that outlines
interconnecting pavilions. Lanai-style living on the shores of Port Douglas
in northeast Australia is enjoyed in true tropical luxury fashion.

urban oasis

Swathed in a mist of green and the humidity that accompanies the
equatorial fervour of Bangkok, this urban retreat has been sensitively
devised by Prabhakorn Vadanyakul to detract as little as possible from
its setting, while ensuring that as much of it is not disturbed – including
the roots of the trees beneath the pool that manages to negotiate its way
around them. Opening out to form a huge veranda, a pivoting wall of glass
draws the inside out to the extraordinary sights and sounds of nature.

living enlightenment

The entrance court to this townhouse in Kuala Lumpur, designed by Ng Sek San, is filled with a creative textural aesthetic and a touch of soul. Like an outdoor living room under the shade of a tree, two armchairs made from wire and concrete are positioned at either end of the pond, while flowering cacti set in wire cages fill the entire wall, like an art installation, adding colour and vitality.

Intending to create a unique dialogue in a space that gives transition between the outer and inner worlds, Ng Sek San explains that the process is also about the enlightenment of the spirit: "The image that constantly comes to mind is the guru sitting under a tree – enlightenment doesn't happen in an enclosed room, it happens outdoors beneath an open sky."

green room *pages 140, 141*

One solution devised by Prabhakorn Vadanyakul to cooling down an interior is an organic approach from the exterior. By letting nature work its magic in order to alleviate and temper the humidity and sunlight, a dense layer of foliage combines with the cooling effects of reflecting pools along this verdant garden path that leads to the swimming pool.

While translucent overhangs shield heavy monsoonal rains, a deck is completely ensconced in the canopies and provides a haven of respite that is deeply grounded in its tropical setting.

tree house

Surrounded by a curtain of nature, a sprawling deck spills out from the interior as the ultimate outdoor room. There's a sense of meditative calm in everything about this weekend retreat, designed by Marcio Kogan. Located high up in the Northern Pantanal of Rio de Janeiro, its smooth modernist lines of concrete, timber and glass fit seamlessly into the environment that's shared with exotic birdlife and the gushing of a stream just below.

decked out *above*

In this beach house designed by Kanika R'Kul on the Gulf of Thailand, a minimal approach to sun worshipping keeps the focus firmly on the setting.

patio scene *opposite*

Rooms and activities move to the exterior and the delights of open-air dining to lounging. On a poolside patio, designed by Jon King, furnishings can be just as laid-back as they are refined, such as this white table setting and sun loungers designed by B&B Italia.

urban bliss *opposite*

Putting the cool into Los Angeles landscaping, the subtle effects of deep grey create fluidity between the external façade, the pool and the idyllic surroundings. Designed by Ron Radziner.

naturally vented *below*

On balmy summer evenings the entrance porch of this Sydney beach house, designed by Tim Roberts, acts as a chimney by channelling hot air up and out through its walls of slatted timber and the security door made from distinctive tapering battens of teak.

integral essence

The pool is every bit as integral to the tropical way of life as the outdoor room is. Here the poolside area of this hinterland hideaway designed by Elizabeth Watson-Brown gives indulgent room to pause, either sitting or enjoying a relaxing swim in the cool of the timber-shaded deck or the water. The pool is enhanced by exotic plants that include such visual delights as frangipani, bougainvillea, banana, bamboo and pawpaw.

the great outdoors

Close to the pristine beaches of Noosa sits a contemporary
dwelling – a hybrid design adopted by Stephen Kidd using
weatherboard cladding and tin roofing to reflect the breezy
vernacular style of the 'Queenslander' bungalow. A dramatic
skillion roof shades a constant flow of family activity while the
deck also converts to a dining room in an ideal setting flanked
by Caribbean date palms and a sprawling pool.

looking glass *above*

An elliptical pool designed by WOHA in
Singapore mirrors the exquisite detailing of
the landscaping where carpet grass lawn is
lifted up above a field of Mondo grass.

coolside *opposite*

A cabana designed by SCDA in Singapore
provides refined poolside lounging that is as
elegantly composed as its surroundings.

water ways *overleaf*

Even with high temperatures, humidity
and the heaviest of monsoonal rains there
remains the need for a connection with nature.
In Singapore outdoor rooms, such as this
poolside retreat designed by SCDA, are made
to relax in. With a timber latticed wall, roughly
hewn sandstone and cooling rattan loungers,
this is the ideal spot in which to sit back and
wait for the storm to subside.

shore appeal *above*
An exhilarating outdoor shower at this bare-foot retreat on the shores of the Gulf of Thailand, designed by Kanika R'Kul.

minimal haven *opposite*
The bold linear strokes of this São Paulo pool setting, designed by Isay Weinfeld, are softened with the undulating curve of a slatted ramp.

clearly defined *page 158*
Overlooking the Nelson Bay hinterland on Australia's east coast, a retreat designed by Gordon & Valich takes in the spectacular scenery.

surface effect *page 159*
In a natural Sydney setting that is clear of deck furniture, the smooth surfaces of western red cedar, blue stone and sandblasted glass form an uninterrupted oasis. Designed by Luigi Rosselli.

natural elements *page 160*
A cabana designed by SCDA in Singapore provides refined poolside lounging that is as elegantly composed as its surroundings.

light box *page 161*
In a light-filled house designed by Simon Carnachan, the focus is on simplicity. With a seamless indoor-outdoor divide, a strong graphic formation is created by pared-back order and consistency throughout the interior to the perfection of the garden, the open-air dining room and the elegant pool.

sightline *above left, left and opposite*
To experience the essence of summer, an endless ocean and the continual flux between the rising and setting of the sun needs only to be accompanied by a minimum of effects. In an oceanfront retreat, designed by Tim Roberts, the experience seems infinite; without so much as a fine divide of glass, there's nothing to separate the vast expanse of the Pacific where water meets the sky.

elements
details, surfaces,
materials,inspiration

planting Maximize the impact of nature with a fresh resolve that begins in the outdoor room –

the most stimulating space of the dwelling.

vivid form

Add a vibrant visual dimension to the soothing sounds of water.

minimal canvas

Form a graphic composition using a little discipline to gain maximum effect.

natural order

Create a dramatic impact by making the most of the simplicity of ordered bands of a living surface.

screen appeal

Where form meets function, shading with external planting will also provide an effective privacy screen – use strong vertical elements such as bamboo.

lush confines

Landscaping reveals the pleasure that can be derived from the simplest of forms.

add the dimension

Wall climbers in all their variations bring life to the canvas of the exterior.

single element

Emphasize a single form of colour to complement the surrounds.

living contrast

Teaming the right colours, tones and textures can lead to richly visual results.

organic geometry

The repetition of creative concepts in simple geometry can make an extraordinary contribution to the outdoor room.

outstanding

The sculptural elements of nature alone are enough to transform any exterior into a sublime landscape.

full bloom

A simple band of vivid colour draws a visual connection from the interior to the garden.

wood
As versatile as it is diverse, wood is as pragmatic in function from a built material to a final finish. Make sure that the wood you choose has been carefully harvested from sustainable forests.

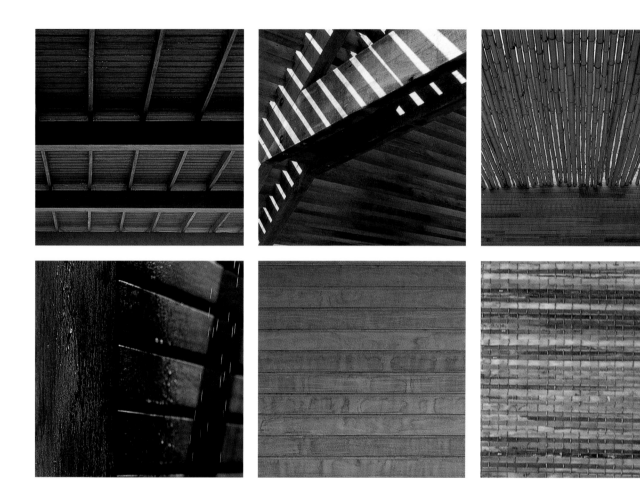

natural resolve

Stable hardwoods, such as teak, cedar and, here, Malaysian teng are incredibly durable and innately moisture-resistant.

cooling angle

The outdoor room needs deeply angled shading to keep the sun at bay.

tactile finish

Wood deepens in character and naturally improves with age. Because it derives from a living source, however, it must be treated with care.

arbour splendour

Pergolas and arbours are the simple yet effective response to a hot climate as well as catering to social needs, providing shelter.

natural weave

The most common rattans are the Calamus species found throughout the Malay peninsula, Indonesia and Vietnam. A palm rather than a grass, it provides a rich textural backdrop.

shaded approach

Bamboo is one of the most versatile, flexible, not to mention eco-friendly hardwoods around.

carving the tradition

Making the most of a creative technique, hand-tooled latticework brings rugged textural warmth to screening.

sound resolve

Enhance the warmth of the living space from an overhead point of view, in this case with cedar battens to line a ceiling.

essential form

A bold interplay between deep shadows forms striking effects.

tactile twist

As the practicalities of veneer don't usually extend to the shower enclosure, richly toned limestone can be just as effective for its tactile appeal.

like-minded

The minimalist ideal is to keep things simple and devote few materials to one space, here Australian tallow, to achieve the ultimate refinement.

rich pickings

Veneers deserve simple, clean design so as not to detract from their natural beauty.

decking
A good landscape scheme ensures that the right materials are chosen to weather the elements as much as to enhance the surrounds.

cutting edge *above*

Minimize the disturbance. While decking is cut to preserve the slender limbs of nature, it can also be illuminated by night with a focus from inlaid spotlights.

industrial elegance *top right*

Industrial grating is multi-purpose, low-maintenance, and more importantly, tough enough to withstand the harshest of environments.

border line *above*

Create a bold definition along the edge of inlaid timber with a textural border such as river pebbles.

bare exposure *above*

When hardwoods are not UV-cured or sealed, like the Brazilian ipé decking used here, they will gracefully weather to a silvered patina when exposed to long periods of direct sunlight.

room to pause *top right*

A design that embraces the locale, that lets us experience the cooling sea breeze and involves us with the surroundings, is considered successful in every respect.

sea life *above*

Where possible it is best to choose local hardwoods that will more readily adapt to the environment. Here the tough durability of Malaysian teng is best equipped to deal with the corrosive elements of the sun, sea air and wind.

screens

Designing ways to catch a breeze, shading and screening out the sun all become an obsession in the tropics – it's all about creating minimal barriers between indoors and the outdoors.

minimal network *above*

A magical space can be made with nothing but slim lines to divide the outdoors. In this case, a fine network of chengal, or Malay teak screens create a simple yet effective way to provide natural ventilation in a room throughout the languid days of year-round warmth.

graphic line *top right*

The strong design elements of a screen wall elongate the interior to dramatic effect.

elegant cedar *above*

Screens reflect a unique and versatile response towards the surrounds. With beautifully crafted design and detailing in wood such as cedar, screens provide the perfect barrier to the sun as they let cooling air continually flow through to the interior.

block-out

With the wealth of natural oils and stains available, any wood surface, in this case marine ply, can achieve richly exotic tones.

screen refinement

Impressive screens provide light control during the day, and by night can act as a breathing skin to the interior.

west side story

A façade is shielded from the intensity of the western sun and traffic noise by a venting-block screen, which is both functional and attractive.

louvred out

Streamline an interior with sleek and sophisticated aluminium louvres that show how climate control can be a breeze.

steel appeal

Fine mesh softens strong light and also has the practical purpose of keeping insects out.

textures

With an eye for a natural composition, minimalism seeks to express the intrinsic beauty of materials – the tone and texture is simply a matter of choice.

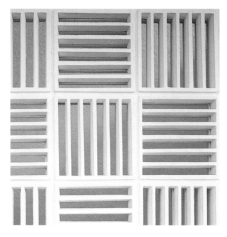

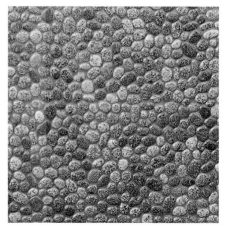

graphic division

Whether to express a style, make a contrast or emphasize a particular material, outdoor room divides provide the perfect opportunity to exercise your creativity.

teak ideal

Create a striking effect by fusing the simplest elements of form with function.

the art of stone

The deep earthy shades of stone provide a tactile approach to making a natural presence felt.

surface attraction

A wall of river-bed pebbles provides a sensual backdrop to a bathroom environment.

artful insight

The minimalist ideal appeals in many different ways.

luscious form *above*

The pure effects of nature are nothing other than sensational.

light play *top right*

The smooth face of honed stone is the perfect surface for light to cast its shadow across.

highlight *above*

Pare back and focus on the pure simplicity of natural elements.

stairs
Stairs are one of the most dramatic elements of the home, defining the minimalist appreciation of the purest and simplest of forms.

glass act

This staircase certainly makes for a dramatic entrance, its treads of smooth marble contributing to a feeling of luxury.

material twist

A spiral staircase can economize on space, create interesting angles and become a feature in its own right.

clear rise

The minimal lines of a seamless staircase provide the perfect canvas backdrop on which to cast an extraordinary light show.

cool rendition

The wedge of space beneath the stairs is often a 'dead' or a transitional space, but in this case it has been transformed into the perfect cooling scene.

natural high

Stairs in sculptural form, here made from cherry wood, can create an impressive visual impact

bare saviour

Hard-wearing stone is practical solution for external stairs. Here bluestone has been chosen to protect bare feet on the way to the paved pool surrounds below.

stair-lit *above*

Importantly, there are simple yet efficient ways to shine the light on stairwells.

climbing refinement *top left*

The magical effects of a floating staircase bring form and function to light.

rising calm *above*

The complete sense of serenity lies in the simple plan of minimalism, and a scrupulous eye for detail.

furniture
With the great rewards of ease, comfort and style, furniture – from sleek and straight to organic shapes and curves – makes its presence felt inside and out.

rolled out

Lay back and soak up the rays on the undulating forms of integral decking.

decked out

Avoid cluttering up the sundeck with this clever integrated design.

reflective haven

A shaded teak bench provides the perfect spot for contemplation.

great escape

In the true spirit of the relaxation refuge, we need nothing more than the essentials to revive.

sheer bliss

The luxury of an integral daybed, laid out to make the most of lush surroundings, allows you to leave all distractions at the door.

tree house

When the day is spent entirely out of doors, a low-key interior is called for to create a space in which to relax.

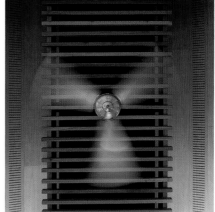

court appeal

The permanent set-up of the outdoor room needs to be as inviting as it is robust and prepared to weather an equatorial climate.

lounged out

The relaxed connection between interior and outdoor spaces enhances the laid-back qualities of furnishings.

inside out

Continue the flow of surface materials to create a seamless connection from the interior to the outdoor room.

essential source

A light airy room allows plenty of space to congregate, as conversation flows around a table that's made to cater for a large crowd.

comfort zone

A high ceiling that provides the soothing whirr of a fan resides in the true fashion of the tropical vernacular.

the integral way

The flow of space happens naturally around integrated, built-in and customized design.

glass

The sheer brilliance of glass presents almost limitless design solutions, whether to capture a view or the breeze – blending the interior of the house seamlessly with the exterior surroundings.

diffusion

Where privacy is paramount, enhance space with the softness of light through a translucent design.

lucid form

Continue the light flow through frosted glass.

light effects

Glass can add a whole new dimension when used cleverly in a design scheme, in this case as it refracts the colour spectrum in the form of sculpture.

angled potential

There is so much potential to bring light into a design when it comprises the brilliant evocations of glass.

liquid rituals

A frosted window wall imparts a haze of softened light while ensuring a complete sense of privacy.

powerful effect

Details that are as receptive to the environment as this make oceanfront living all the more intimate.

pause for reflection

Simply gazing at the horizon instils a sense of tranquillity from any aspect, although it will always be more evocative if you do so through the seamless clarity of glass.

nature inspired

Like its smooth transition between interior and the exterior environment, the careful use of glass and glazing further adds to the luxurious ambience of this waterfront haven.

windows
Windows frame a continual experience through the diverse angles of clever

louvres and slots that cross-ventilate to sweeping expanses of glazing, using a view to powerful effect.

sheer intimacy

Experience the pleasure of feeling

at one with nature from the inside.

tall order

Louvres create the all-important
airflow through the interior with
cross-ventilation.

clearly framed

Choose framing materials either to
contrast or integrate with the design with
both interior and exterior of the home.

means of control

There are many fresh ways in which
to control the passage of air and light.

details count

Circular elements such as this bring
a unique appeal to detail.

colour
Colour plays a main role in promoting the mood as it takes – be it a sense of calm through natural tones, harmony with hues that refer to the landscape or striking a balance with the bold.

  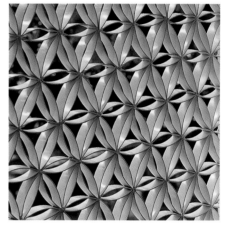

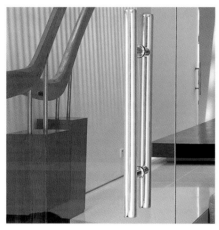  

tantalize

Man-made composite materials offer a whole colour spectrum of choice.

beside art

Juxtapose art or ornament carefully to complement the surrounds.

water ways

Bring water to life – fish, eight gold and one black, will activate the best in feng shui.

glass appeal

There is a jewel-like richness of colour to be discovered among the merits of glass mosaic.

design frame

Look at a fresh perspective through the collage of a filigree screen.

wildlife

Arrange the exotic delights of the tropics with abandon.

calm elegance

Harmonize and translate the subtle hues of natural materials through furnishing upholstery and cushions.

energize

Inject emotion with paint, the most lucrative of colour tools.

natural outlook

Introduce a view to nature and grow a screen of luscious foliage.

tactile influence

Sensual tones and textures complement one another.

hot seat

Begin with a stark canvas to express a creative desire.

magical moments

Invite colour that lingers.

pools

Bring the reflective, seductive allure of water into line with an equally bold and simple expression – and take the plunge.

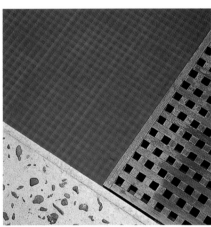

elliptical effects

The complete calm of a minimalist landscape is found here through a strong concept of linear form and materials that complement the entire scene.

deep end

The pool setting is the ultimate place in which to define the ideal minimal juxtaposition of materials.

natural cool

Deep shade in a warm climate is created effectively with foliage that persists throughout the year.

cutting edge

Water brims over a solid outline of granite that creates the perfect seamless edge.

pool house

From laps to naps, the pursuit of recreation all takes place at the edge of the dream idyll of home.

soothing motion

Adding a splash to a tranquil scene provides interest and emphasizes the feeling of coolness .

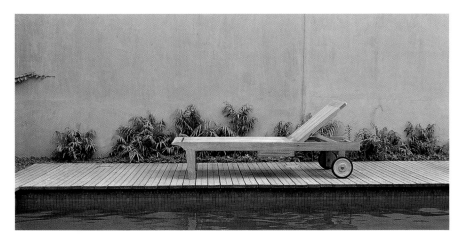

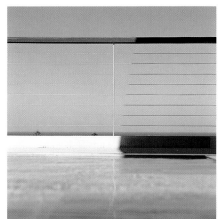

simple order

A contrasting scheme plays out
smooth concrete against a vibrant
splash of cobalt.

ideal seclusion

A perimeter wall creates the perfect
enclosure to an intimate pool scene.

reflective style

A timber balustrade forms a sleek
outline to shimmering body of water.

design icon

Bring life to the poolside with stylish,
carefully chosen furnishings.

optical effects

Reinvent the natural scheme in the
water itself, or in the landscaping,
at dusk to a magic effect.

architects and designers

Andrew Lister Architect

PO Box 91793

Auckland Mail Centre

Auckland

New Zealand

T + 64 9 307 7050

E andrewlister@mac.com

www.andrewlisterarchitect.com

bloc design

5 Eurella Street

Kenmore

Queensland 4069

Australia

T + 61 7 3720 2342

F + 61 7 3720 2341

www.blocdcl.com

Crosson Clarke Carnachan Architects

33 Bath Street

Parnell

Auckland

New Zealand

T + 64 9 379 7234

F + 64 9 379 7235

www.carnachan-architects.co.nz

CSA Architects Pty Limited

185 Old South Head Road

Bondi Junction

NSW 2022

Australia

T + 61 2 9389 4055

F + 61 2 9389 4077

E alex@csa-arch.com.au

www.csa-arch.com.au

Dawson Brown Architecture Pty Ltd

Level 1, 63 William Street

East Sydney

NSW 2010

Australia

T + 61 2 9360 7977

F + 61 2 9360 2123

E dba@dawsonbrownarchitecture.com

www.dawsonbrownarchitecture.com

Design King Company Pty Ltd

102/21 Alberta Street

Sydney

NSW 2000

Australia

P + 61 2 9261 3062

F + 61 2 9261 3175

E jonking@netspace.net.au

www.designking.com.au

Duangrit Bunnag Architect Limited

(dbalp)

989 Floor 28 Unit A2-B3 Siam Tower

Rama 1 Road, Patumwan

Bangkok 10330

Thailand

T + 66 2 658 0580-1

F + 66 2 658 0582

E duangrit@loxinfo.co.th

Elizabeth Watson Brown Architects

88 Gailey Road

St. Lucia

Queensland 4067

Australia

T + 61 7 3870 7760

F + 61 7 3870 4752

E info@ewbarchitects.com

www.ewbarchitects.com

Fearon Hay Architects Ltd

PO Box 90311, AMSC

Level 2, 20 Beaumont Street

Freemans Bay, Auckland

New Zealand

T + 64 9 309 0128

F + 64 9 309 0827

E contact@fearonhay.com

www.fearonhay.com

Giovanni D'Ercole

Love and Hatred

Shop 79

Level 1, The Strand Arcade

George Street

Sydney

NSW 2000

Australia

T + 61 2 9233 3441

E info@loveandhatred.com.au

www.loveandhatred.com.au

Gordon & Valich Architects

105 Reservoir Street

Surry Hills

NSW 2010

Australia

T + 61 2 9212 1599

F + 61 2 9212 3053

E info@gordonvalich.com.au

www.gordonvalich.com.au

Jahn Associates Architects

Level 1

105 Reservoir Street

Surry Hills

NSW 2010

Australia

T + 61 2 9211 2191

F + 61 2 9211 2161

E studio@jahn.com.au

www.jahn.com.au

Kerry and Lindsay Clare

41 McLaren Street

North Sydney

NSW 2060

Australia

T + 61 2 9929 0522

F + 61 2 9959 5765

www.architectus.com.au

Koning Eizenberg Architecture

1454, 25th Street

Santa Monica, CA 90404

USA

T + 1 310 828 6131

F + 1 310 828 0719

E info@kearch.com

www.kearch.com

Inspace

PO Box 1989

Byron Bay, NSW 2481

Australia

T + 61 2 6685 5296

F + 61 2 6680 8927

E in_space@bigpond.com

Isay Weinfeld Architect

Rua André Fernandes 175

Itaim-Bibi

São Paulo, SP 04536-020

Brazil

T + 55 11 3079 7581

F + 55 11 3079 5656

E info@isayweinfeld.com

www.isayweinfeld.com

JMA ARCHITECTS

Level 1

PO Box 380

Spring Hill

Brisbane 4004

Australia

T + 61 7 3839 3794

F + 61 7 3839 6112

www.jma-arch.com

JONES SONTER

PO Box 483

Rozelle

NSW 2039

Australia

T + 61 2 9555 7464

F + 61 2 9555 7463

E mail@jonesonter.com.au

www.jonesonter.com.au

Judy Houlton - Interior Designer

Sydney

Australia

T + 61 4 1825 0390

E judyhoulton@optusnet.com.au

Louise Nettleton Architect Pty Ltd

Studio 56

61 Marlborough Street

Surry Hills

NSW 2010

Australia

T + 61 2 9318 0428

F + 61 2 9318 2419

E mail@nettletonarchitect.com

Lamond Building

52 Hopetoun Avenue

Mosman

Sydney

NSW 2088

Australia

T + 61 4 1825 2701

F + 61 2 9960 5568

E glamond@bigpond.net.au

Luigi Rosselli Pty Ltd

15 Randle Street

Surry Hills

NSW 2010

Australia

T + 61 2 9281 1498

F + 61 2 9281 0196

E luigirosselli@netspace.net.au

www.luigirosselli.com

Marcio Kogan

Al Tietê 505

São Paulo

SP 01417-020

Brazil

T + 55 11 3081 3522

F + 55 11 3063 3424

E mk-mk@uol.com.br

www.marciokogan.com.br

Marmol Radziner + Associates AIA

12210 Nebraska Avenue

Los Angeles, CA 90025

USA

T + 1 310 826 6222

F + 1 310 826 6226

E info@marmol-radziner.com

www.marmol-radziner.com

Ngiom Partnership

D30, 3rd Floor, Block D

Plaza Pekeliling

Jalan Tun Razak

Kuala Lumpur 50400

Malaysia

T + 60 3 4043 4833

F + 60 3 4041 3833

E ngiom@ngiom.com

Chad Oppenheim

245NE 37th Street s102

Miami,

Florida 33137

USA

T + 1 305 576 8404

F + 1 305 576 8433

E chad@oppenoffice.com

www.oppenoffice.com

SCDA Architects Pte Ltd

10 Teck Lim Road

Singapore 088386

T + 65 6324 5458

F + 65 6324 5450

E scda@starhub.net.sg

www.scdaarchitects.com

Seksan Design

67 Jalan Tempinis Satu

Lucky Garden

Bangsar

Kuala Lumpur 59100

Malaysia

T + 60 3 2282 4611

F + 60 3 2882 0366

E mail@seksan.com

www.seksan.com

Small Projects

1 Jalan Tenggiri

Kuala Lumpur 59100

Malaysia

T + 60 3 2200 1800

F + 60 3 2282 2861

E lsd@pd.jaring.my

www.small-projects.com

Spacetime Architects

4th Floor, 32 Soi Soonvijai 8 [3]

Petchburi Road

Bangkapi, Huaykwang

Bangkok 10320

Thailand

T + 66 2 7181 5333 5

F + 66 2 318 7717

E admin@spacetime.co.th

Stephen Collins

SCID Pty Ltd

Suite 28, Level 3

151 Bayswater Road

Rushcutters Bay

NSW 2011

Australia

T + 61 2 9356 8179

F + 61 2 9356 8174

E stephen@scid.com.au

Stephen Kidd

Kidd & Co Designers

PO Box 262

Noosa Heads

Queensland 4567

Australia

T + 61 7 5447 5633

F + 61 7 5447 5833

E stephen@kiddco.com.au

www.kiddco.com

Steven Ehrlich Architects

10865 Washington Boulevard

Culver City, CA 90232

USA

T + 1 310 838 9700

F + 1 310 838 9737

E info@s-ehrlich.com

www.s-ehrlich.com

Tim Roberts Design

PO Box 335

Malvern

Victoria 3144

Australia

T + 61 3 9500 8852

F + 61 3 9500 0469

E info@tim-roberts.com

www.tim-roberts.com

Toshiko Mori Architect

180 Varick Street, Suite 1322

New York, NY 10014

USA

T + 1 212 337 9644

F + 1 212 337 9647

E staff@tmarch.com

www.tmarch.com

Prabhakorn Vadanyakul

81 Sukhumvit 26

Bangkok 10110

Thailand

T + 66 2 2260 4370

F + 66 2 2259 3872

E a49@a49.com

www.a49.com

Warren and Mahoney Limited

201 Victoria Street West

PO Box 91517

Auckland

New Zealand

T + 64 9 309 4894

F + 64 9 309 2671

E wam@wam.co.nz

www.warrenandmahoney.com

WOHA Designs Pte Ltd

175 Telok Ayer Street

Singapore 068623

T + 65 6423 4555

F + 65 6423 4666

E admin@wohadesigns.com

www.wohadesigns.com

x squared design P/L

498 Darling Street

Balmain, NSW 2041

Australia

T + 61 2 9810 8255

Acknowledgments

For our son and daughter, Maximilian and Mia Isabella

With our warmest thanks to all of the owners around the world who welcomed us into their homes – we are truly humbled.

Our deepest appreciation goes to the following architects and designers for their contributions and invaluable insight into the world of Tropical Minimal, and whose work is the inspiration that fills these pages. Australia: Rob Brown, Kerry and Lindsay Clare, Stephen Collins, Giovanni D'Ercole, Bruce Hanlee, Judy Houlton, Graham Jahn, Kim Jones, Stephen Kidd, Jon King, Greg Lamond, John Mainwaring, Warren Naylor, Peter Nelson, Louise Nettleton, Susan Reed, Tim Roberts, Luigi Rosselli, Alex Smith, Elizabeth Watson-Brown and Furio Valich; Brazil: Marcio Kogan and Isay Weinfeld; New Zealand: Robyn and Simon Carnachan, Scott Koopman, Andrew Lister, Jeff Fearon and Tim Hay; Malaysia: Kevin Low, Ng Seksan and Lim Teng Ngiom; Singapore: Chan Soo Khian, Richard Hassell and Wong Mun Summ; Thailand: Prabhakorn Vadanyakul, Duangrit Bunnag and Kanika R'Kul; USA: Steven Ehrlich, Julie Eizenberg and Hank Koning, Scott Hughes, Toshiko Mori, Chad Oppenheim and Ron Radziner. Thank you to our editor, Lucas Dietrich, firstly for his inspiration and trust, and then for his patience.

We are hugely grateful to Kerry Hill of Kerry Hill Architects, Karen McCartney at Inside Out, David Clark at *Vogue Living*, Clarissa Schneider at *Casa Vogue Brazil* and Jannine Mezrani for offering their support and generosity of time. Thanks are also due to the following Australian magazines, for allowing us to publish Richard's images previously commissioned by: *Vogue Living*, *Inside Out* and *Home Beautiful*, and to Saskia Havekes of Grandiflora, Sydney for supplying the perfect orchids. And to Helene, Gilian and Maurice our sincerest thanks for their continuous care and encouragement.

First published in the United Kingdom in 2006 by Thames & Hudson Ltd, 181A High Holborn, London WC1V 7QX

www.thamesandhudson.com

© 2006 Thames & Hudson Ltd, London
Photographs © 2006 Richard Powers
Texts © 2006 Danielle Miller

British Library Cataloguing-in-Publication Data
A catalogue record for this book is available from the British Library

ISBN-13: 978-0-500-51291-3
ISBN-10: 0-500-51291-4

Printed in Singapore by CS Graphics